everything was permanent

and nothing changed

To my father:
who always makes sure life is our best dream.
never stops thinking about others, first.
thank you for always being there.
for giving us your everything
even when we had nothing.
Thank you.

To my mother:
the strongest woman I know.
who wants to protect us from
all that is bad in this world.
been through more than she should,
and still manages to guide us
with a face of courage.
Thank you.

I owe the world to you both.

I love you.

A Brief Autobiography.

4. Fol oh the dots. fall-o the rules. a life in a box be gun. Flag is raisd and pried ingravd. Indonesian born and (half) bred.

5. Yes. No. I love you. Got it? Go.
Can you speek inglish? Yes. No.
Is this your first skool? Yes. No.
What's your name? Mm. Hum. name. nama.
Achintya! A.Chin.Tia. A-chin, Tia. Tia. I love you!
A perfect score. and more. Best of the best. Top of the top.

6. Okay now start again. You are fluent now yes?
Achi, achinn, Achincha? No just Tia.
Tia.
Eesy peesy lemon squeezy.
Liar liar pants on fire.

7. I know you are but what am I.
What am I.

Girls and Boys can't be friends!

"A sailor went to C C C,"
"A sailor went to.. Dizz Knee Land."

8. Kapacity is K a p a c i t y.
"Sorry, do you want to try again?"
K a p a c i t y.
"Sorry, you're out."
Out of the game.
Next, expelled.
Next, disappointment.
Next, not loved.

"C a p a c i t y" A smirk flung, and hate erupted.
Rivalry was born.

9. "Apples on a stick just makes me sick, just makes my heart beat 2 forty six.

Now close your eyes and count to ten. 1, 2, 3, 4, 5, 6, 7, 8, 9, 10"
You're my best friend. First friend, With no end. So forever and ever. Best Friends Forever.

Funny. Athletic. Saxophone. Oh boy, a boy.
"Tya has a crush on youuu" Girls. are. mean.

But boys and girls can't be friends!

What class are you? What class what class what class? 5a? 5b. 5 bummed you are not in my class.

10. Here's a pen. Now lets be friends.

Smarter. Smarter. Smartest.
You're going to let some white girl beat you?
Faster. Faster. Fastest.
98%? That's the best you can do?

Best friend Bullies, Best friend Bullied.
Are we,
still friends?

"Hey can I join you?" No.
Can she join you? "Yes!"
Separation. Click.
Weirdo. Ugly. Click Click.
"You have boys shoes."
"Why do you tie your hair like that?"
Layers of confidence shed like an onion.

Apparently "Cheese!" mean pose.
And not Smile Your Widest Grin.

Girls are so mean.
But girls and boys can't be friends.

Off the bike, and out of uniform, we are goin' to the jungle kids!

"Good morning, Good morning"

Best of the best.
Well, that was easy.

Worms can be farmed?
Wait.
Animals at school?

11. super green super camp.
A friend. A boy?
A friend.

12. Middle School.
We're with the bigger kids now.
Whole set of new rules here.
Girls can't dress like that anymore. The boys are looking. But yes, they still have "cooties."

Best friend is back. Back in Business.

"Will you go out with me" becomes a catchphrase.
And the automatic response is "no."
How does one say "It's not because I don't like you, it's because my mum doesn't let me. Not until I'm in college."

In middle school we learn: that family members die. And this brings people closer closer, just close enough to stand next to each other, but not close enough to see the tears fall down.
A mourning mother mourns her mother. While children orbit her like sombre headless chickens. Interesting to know flames consume *almost* everything, but not *everything* there is still some of grandma left. She is there you see, in that container, just squatting and watching, waiting.

Also. women must be too fragile to have sea legs. So it is okay that they stand back to watch, as the men sail away to C, C, C and gently, delicately let grandma in her container sink.

Looking around and seeing 1, 2, all and more.
"Hi do you remember me? You were only young."
"Say hi."
"Show respect."
"Is that how you do it?*ahah*"
Translation: Is that how I taught you to do it.

Family has always been here. But here is only when here is needed.

13. Teen Ager.
A friend. A boy?
A boy-friend.
Let's hold hands. Culturally that's okay. But in the West (not) Stern world that is not enough.
Not good enough.

Life became a list.
D for Don't show your love in public.
Don't kiss him.
Decided to not be together.
Dad's not home again.
Divorce is looming lengthy.
Deep Sadness not Depression.
Because Depression doesn't exist!

Falling Falling in thoughts.
Falling Falling and oh! There's a net called family.
Has that always been there?
Again "Family will always be there."

The thought of peaceful escape called death.

And the strength in Cowardice.

"Look, your dad sometimes.."
"You see, your mom sometimes…"

"You are not West (not) Stern. You were raised here, are living here, you are Indonesian born and bred (only half!)."

Quest means journey. Which means road. With a bridge to

14. The BIG kids.
The High school.
Where things got hard not because of the work load, but the constant
thought
thought
thought
that everyone is looking, everyone is judging, everyone is waiting to see what moments they can snatch up to spin into hideous ridiculous rumours.
Expectations are lifted, but not work wise, more "do you have a boyfriend? how old? good looking? nice?" "Do you drink? how much? lightweight?"
"are you… you know..?"
what.
"you know.."
oh.

Learning that sometimes saying yes can lead to consequences.
Like being around people you don't like.

Understanding that thoughts spiral.
They drag you down.
They twist the truths and spit out lies.
They crowd your mind AND SOMETIMES THEY SHOUT.

but their truest evil is this.
come close.
it's a whisper.

They only speak to *you*.
and take shelter in your mind.
Because out here,
it doesn't exist.

15. Jagged tumbling of emotions broken by a moment of clarity.

A Love Unknown. Or not wanting to be Known.
Because right now is too young.
Too inexperienced to wholly encompass an emotion so deep.
So play along. Pretend that it's just "I really really l…l…like you" and nothing more than that.
Like it has nothing to do with the fact that the voices are QUIET QUIet quieting.
As if Love's eyes, Love's voice, touch, laugh, whisper was nothing but that.
Eyes, a voice, a touch, whisper and laugh.
But let the feeling build and build like the shaking of a soda can and just almost just before it goes, pop the top and

nothing.

Love fizzles out.
The mind has gone mute.
and the self has become an empty vessel,
too much gone to even be able to wonder how and why.
It
Is
Lonely.

Like a calm before the storm.
And the storm came in the form of.

Death.

It is Dad's little brother but what is felt is Tya's little sister.
Empathy is a bitch.
But be strong, be strong
until you stub your toe and burst in tears.
"God it hurts" it hurts that people leave your life
like a candle being snuffed out.
Suddenly, and without warning.

A clomp, half-clomp up the stairs and sniffled crawling onto bed.

The ceiling seems to breathe with the thoughts.

IN: It's Deep Sadness not Depression. Depression is too deep too strong to unbelievably unaccepted to be real.
OUT: Imprisoned mind > In prison, confined.

IN: wondering how Love is doing and why won't he speak during a time as tough as this.
OUT: "Romeo, Romeo, wherefore art thou Romeo?"

IN: "Wake me up when it's all over" songs being tainted by memories of people. as if the song could keep them alive just for a little bit longer please.
OUT: can never listen to this song again.

IN: each breath is a struggle
OUT: exhales interrupted by shattered sobs

IN: everything looks blurred and underwater
OUT: when will the torrent of tears end?

IN: The funeral is 11764km away
OUT: Is this a metaphor for the distance between Us and Them. The half bred, not quite a part.

16. Three little planets are going out of orbit. And a mother moon is trying to reign them in.
"That's not how I treated my parents."
"If I was your age doing that, my parents would have."
"You are still Indonesian."

Three little planets orbited by the father sun. and the heat is a shelter attempting to encircle all of everything marked DANGER!
"It's okay. I'll handle everything."
"No, no we're doing fine."
"The advantage of coming from a mixed family is..."

What? What.
How come this little planet is the only one who doesn't get it?
How come this little planet is the only one who seems to feel the darkness and coldness of space.
"It's just forced thoughts in your head."
"If you think yourself out of it you'll be fine."
How can polar opposites of a culture have such similar thoughts on thought.
That it only exists in your mind and you can change it as easily as putting a different shirt on.
Like getting out of bed is just a one foot after the other. Carry your mind with you! It's not that heavy. Are you really that weak?

Deep Sadness not Depression.

Poetic lines give voice to what is whispered.
A mind battered by an anthem. "Mental Illness is not valid."
Sung both sun and moon and sister planets.

Hiding in suffocation, because the Politically Correct Police are around. Buzzing "Hey don't joke about that, people actually suffer from that."
Right right.
Tya has it easy.
Easy peasy. peachy fuzz. Fuzzy is the way to speak because it turns people away.
And away is good. Right?
Suffering, if not real, must be dealt with alone.

Friends fell like flies.
"She's just kind of selfish."
"I don't know, kind of really annoying."

Did you hear about the party you were not invited to? Oh yeah everyone is going. No no, you don't count as anyone.
Obviously.
Otherwise you would have been on the invite list.

Not a big deal,
not a big deal.
"Family is always here."
But here when here is needed.

Moon calling. Because "You are Indonesian born and bred."

But sun is orbiting West (not) Stern.

17. Dancing Queen. Swaying alone.
A birthday spent in tears because nobody seems to get that.
that.
just.

Acceptance is a world being lifted off the shoulders.

Thought is shared to one, and that is one enough to share the burden. To walk the shaky path broken, but leaning on each other. With the devil on their back, and Eden on the horizon.

The demons in the mind must be kept at bay, or the self gets sent away.
The demons in the mind must be unthunk, or the self is a piece of junk.
Two clashing cultures merging on their thoughts of thought.

Escape is futile, so swim with the current and not against it.
Understanding that emptiness sometimes means feeling too much.
Just getting good at shutting out.

Vulnerability has a death penalty. Maybe. Probably. Nobody knows, because there's no such thing.

"Your family is having a wedding. This only happens once."

"Your family is having a wedding. This only happens once."

In the beginning, the wish was that escape is as easy as a firework leaving the ground, and dying in the sky. Goodbye now! I won't be back, thank god! Not looking forward to death, no, just waiting for

—inexistence.

But at the end, we're left with

Lessons learned:

- Mental ill-not.
- Family is top priority, top security, but bottom of the pyramid.
- Love is a promise.
- Promises are made to be broken.
- Sexuality, Sex-Dual-lity good god! Can you imagine such a thing!
- The future is like a non-newtonian fluid. It slips through fingers if not held tight enough.
- The little things, the happy things
- Time is fear and fear is time.
- Life does not accelerate, it spins and spins and it goes so fast, too fast and suddenly it's the edge of a cliff.
on the brink of

Till Death Do Us (Part I).

She is walking down the stairs.
step,
step,
a twisted foot a tumble far.
The soft sound of a cracked neck and the
plump-plump-plump of a limp body rolling down
each step.

Tragic.

She shook the thought away.

We associate songs with places, moments and memories.

80s Love Songs
reminds me of car rides with my mum,
Because it's the only songs she and I can both sing along to.

Bohemian Rhapsody is a 3am drizzle and singing our hearts out on a New York rooftop because the speakers had run out of battery.

Golden, brings with it an image of Swedish highways, and the curve of a road that hugs the water. It is the sun beyond, outlining a shimmering silhouette around his face. One hand on the wheel, and another intertwined with my restless fingers.

We associate people with things, moments and points of growth.

I could dance for the first time
without care with you.
Because you made every awkward shamble of mine into a new and innovative dance move.
Limbs all over, a face pained from laughter.

I learned to take action for the things I want, for the things I love
when your lack of one motivated me to do so.

You taught me that friends can let you down again and again and again yet still expect your apology.

And you else taught me to never lose hope, and to still trust in people despite.

We are the epitome of all our past experiences.

You must think:

Uncage me.
Let me strike the world.

If I am
Sad

If I am one of
The Sad

Then we
are just clouds in a
pain-filled sky

If you were listening,
Perhaps you'd have seen
the broken behind the smile.

I am the fish that gets reeled in, unhooked, thrown back into the ocean

When the memory simmers to a forgotten place the line gets tossed in again.

I should've known you
were just like the rest of them.

Bring me to your home,
Not where you live,
but where you feel your heart rests.
Where you feel the most alive.
Where you save a small space
For just right,
To tuck themselves in.

In between the slices of light, there you'll find me locked in my own darkness. Trapped in the hope of a better tomorrow, unable to release the chains of my past.

Little thoughts:

Just passed by the moon and I thought it was a set light.

12am.

The night: is young
All of us: are young
We will not: be young
                      like this,
                      forever.

Swift zig zags through sparse streets.

The noise of the car
The night
The air

Breathing in tune with the
Press of the acceleration
The dark laughs with you.

laughter, background, conversation.
Noise surrounding.
Moment elapsing
Nostalgia creeping

A piercing realization that this
is happy, and this
is fleeting, and this
you live in and through anyway.

It takes <u>just one</u> moment of abandonment
for <u>any one</u> to feel abandoned for life.

                        - friends for a minute.

There's always that one person that stops breath,
reason, time.

The one that always seems to draw you in.
Your entire world.
The
center of your existence.

You look at them,
And it's like everything else is out of focus.
Just background noise.

That's how you know.

The one:

When you know, you know (?)

Slowly as time spent elapses or at first sight.

Do you believe in —
Love:

Slowly slide into the water
or jump off the cliff?

Does one:
Slide into love

or is it:
a head on collision

— at first sight?

Till Death Do Us (Part II).

Walking along the muddy
lot she looks up
at the
tropical canopy.

Leaves filter sunlight etching barcodes on skin.

Out of pure coincidence
a coconut drops
and her vision
narrows.

It is accelerating but everything
seems slower.
The bulbous seed smacks her face
and splatters
fresh red runny juice of life.

The honk of a car shattered her thoughts.

The taste of freedom sky.
Flight.
Taking flight.

Something we all wish to do.
But not unlike a bird, embody the spread wings and the feeling of the wind beneath.

No, more like,

The way laughter feels on your chest as you're driving through empty streets at 4 in the morning with all your favorite people around you.

The sigh of burdens being lifted as the final sentence is typed on an essay due in the next few hours.

When the wheels of the plane skid across the tarmac, a whoosh of the brakes sending this vehicle to a halt, and the rush that runs through your veins.
You are home.

The tug at your heart watching your father laugh with his sister his brother his mother.

Watching your mother smile.

The flight I speak of is the taste of Love and Beauty the way it is meant to be felt.
An all encompassing underlay to life.
Omnipresent.

We are all unique, but we can also learn from each other's experiences —
And use that knowledge to better understand ourselves.

The walk.

Trees a silhouette grasping for the sky
Tangled twisty limbs reach in
It is dark but I am glowing

Snow falling in a snow globe kind of landscape.
Freckles in the sky dust the trees
Coat the coats
Dissolve on hair, on face
On hands held tight for warmth.

A path trodden being tread
The crunch of boots on snow
The hum of your voice
A buzz on my skin

This. is the first instance.

List of things that make me smile:

- Goats
- Cows chewing with their eyes closed
- toddlers attempting to run
- airplane, landing, home
- soulful instrumental solos

- when you said "hey you"
- your smile
- your voice
- your laugh

- the thought of you
- you

- leaves falling
- snow falling

   I am falling

Do you ever start to unconsciously mimic the facial expressions of those you spend the most time with?

It is the light of the heavens that escapes through your eyes.

pause.

God,

Take me back into your fiery embrace.

All these souls are drawn to you.

We are tired.

It's been a long journey.

Little thoughts:

Apartment lights winking off like dominoes.

The silence is chilling.
Hair on skin rising,
Goosebumps shimmer into existence.

It is luring me.
Wispy fingers curl in a call.

You know you don't want to — dive.
You know you can't help yourself — regardless.

Fall.
Fall deeply.
Fall into this spiraling slumber.

It seems to say.

Tasting the abyss on the edge of your mind,
Reasoning with the madness of release.

Perhaps,

It wouldn't be so bad.

The Imaginary:

I want our song.

Our running around trying to create romance.

Candles, roses, in baths.

Vacations by the beach.
On a remote island.
In a bungalow.

Flowers.

A text Goodmorning, A text Goodnight,
A text, "I'm thinking of you."

Moonlit dinners cooking each other's favourites.

Lying underneath the stars
Spontaneous road trips
An "I Love You" in every continent.

I want what the movies tell and the books write.
The fairytale romance.

The Real:

It was a dreary Monday afternoon
A stormy sky and cold winds draped over the city
A fierce hurricane of thoughts battered around in
my mind, coating the bliss of your presence.
"Can I just get ice cream and a bath," I said.
"That sounds like a very good plan, let's get you
home then," You replied.

We're at Baskin Robins and I tell you how when my
sister and I were kids, whenever we could afford
something slightly luxurious we would get a pint of
Pralines n' Cream and Mint Chocolate Chip,
because those were the two flavours we could agree
on as a collective favourite.
They only had Pralines n' Cream that day.

The day before your flight I had made some pasta
with two separate sauces because you "don't like the
texture of mushrooms."
You attempted to discreetly shove something into
the freezer.
"What is that" I said.
"It's a secret" You replied.
Surprisingly, I managed to tackle my way into
grabbing the bag.
(You'll say it's because you let me.)

It was a plastic Dunkin' Doughnuts cup filled to the
brim with Mint Chocolate Chip ice cream.

Somehow, I love this tale more.

We met once,
Briefly.

And then we were telling mirrored stories
of our childhood.

Separate,
But infused with similarities.

Your two worlds so vastly different from my own,
and yet,
Why then did our parents commit acts identical to
each other. As if following the same script.

Perhaps, it is only in biological imprints that we
humans suffer a difference.

In reality, we're all just stumbling our way through,
similarly alone,
similarly wanting to be a part of something,
together.

Alone together.

Two halves of one mind:

1. Why is it so hard to be me.
Why can't I just have a normal-wired mind.

2. (because super people aren't meant to be ordinary)

Till Death Do Us (Part III).

The wheels on the bus go round
Not slowing
The walking man is red meaning
Do not go.

She steps,
On paved path stripped to signal crossing
Timed in synchronicity
As heated metal, front of the vehicle
Rams her side
Up in the air, to the infinite and beyond.

She lands in a splayed display of broken bones and leaking flesh.
Her brain is a bowl of cherries.
Onlookers screaming and whispering at the deliberate chaos.

The brush of a shoulder reels her thoughts back in focus.

Hey You,

When the sky has turned alluring

Your voice a velvet song

Our empty glasses clinking

A classic radio voice drones on…

I can only be a moon.
So find me the light of my sun.

You can spend months and feel only a slight pull
Or it can take three days to be
completely utterly deeply
fallen

You were a turning point in my life.

I loved myself, the way I am, after you.

You, are the one I compare them to.

And maybe,
                 - I'll always be writing about you.

But wait.

Now there's you.

The second love.

Yet, I have given more of myself to you than I have to anyone else before.

And I am scared.
And I am rejuvenated.
And now I know.

You never forget the first love,
But that doesn't mean you won't love like this again.

Cozy Homes and Comfort Held.

Fuzzy Socks and Warm Tea kind of love.

A smile that melts the heart, like butter.
Dimples sweet as sugar.
A sugar high my chest explodes.
and I
am
addicted.

Soothing strums on Bass surrounds
the sound is humming
Is tuned
to the vibrations of a soul blinded by love.

A stolen glance, a glance some more,
A deep settled look unsettling
Me and My Thoughts
shatter

I cannot think

You have taken my breath away,
Always taking my breath away.

Seems I am not done with bleeding cheesy poems into existence.

Not wanting to let go of each other,
But knowing we have to leave each other,
Is the worst kind of breakup.

Plane rides train rides car rides.
Closing distances for our love.

Museums walked, psychology talk,
Volcanoes climbed with a view, sublime.
Running in the rain for pizza overflowing with toppings,
Walking hand in hand through empty streets as the sun, rises in the distance,
A bridge, crossed
In a literal sense,
In a cultural sense,
In a we are both so new at this oh god what are we doing, sense.

There is so much love here, it is overwhelming.
and I am pained at the thought that, our paths, do not wish to intertwine.

My living-life-in-a-fairytale shattered when you uttered those words in the car that one day, bringing reality crashing down upon us.
Perhaps we could figure it out, test the waters, align a future — compromised.

But I think, my love, it would hurt less
to simply say,
goodbye.

When you have found a love like ours
it is hard to see anyone in color again.

They are grey,
and you,
my ever vibrant flame.

Dear Love,

I see forever in you.
The way I saw forever in him.
But more so in the one before him.

I am always seeing forever
in whoever is my present tense.
In the one who occupies my mind right now.
My right now.
My Right, now.

So how real is my forever really?
If each reality is my new real.

Did I move on too quick
Have I not moved on at all?

Because.
Each one of you knows a different part of me.
Each one takes a different part of me.
But always,
Each one creates a newer part of me.

Am I simply stacking parts of me?

In preparation for that final other half of me.
Who is that whole, that other, the last, my end?
Who are you? I ask. Who am I, without you?
Am I, without you?

Who am I?

You open like an unfurling leaf.
Delicate. Fragile. Tentative.
A smiling curl of innocence.

The first to hurt you, is like a piece of you ripped.
Sharp. Stinging. Sorrow.
A feeling unexpected, wind knocked out of chest.

You retract.
Fragmented.
And then.

The first to hurt you deeply, is like being picked completely off the stem.
Imbalanced. Detached. Untethered.
A crippling sense of endlessly falling through empty space.

Little Thoughts:

This city is pumping blood into a dying corpse.

Everlasting Nights.

The thumping rhythmic noise, vibrations in your chest, a booming blast of clamorous sounds.

Turned down.

The party trickles out and around
Spaces widening, broadening, breathing deepening.

As the night fades, conversations are fading, and memories have faded,.

A crowd dispersed,
We are the stragglers.
desperately try to cling
on to what is left
of a moment spent without thought.
without worry.
without a care for what tomorrow will bring
for what is tomorrow?

When we are held in this blissful time,
A sliver of suspended time,
Smeared, in utter happiness.

The night lingers on.

The girl everyone feels a connection to.

because of her voice,
> her resonating presence.

And when you have her tuned to you,

it is like,

the galaxies have just shifted
> to revolve around you.

Till Death Do Us (Part IV).

She sits in the car,
the voices drone in
the background and
the vehicles
buzz by.
In front is an overflow
of metal beams
with a truck squeezed underneath.

She tilts her head in time
with the pierce of a screeching scream,
unsure if it came from
the brakes or her mother's mouth.

Metal through
glass, through
skin flesh and bone, through
foam seat and it
got tired there.

The sound of panic
spins and blares the surrounding as
her eyes and mouth
flutter in unison.

The yell of her name drags her back to reality.

"I really want to just sit next to you and annoy you"

It's funny how
there's that one person
Your brain circles back to

Maybe that's why they say you never forget your
first love.

No, that's not right.

I thought,
you don't forget,
but,
that doesn't mean you won't love like that again.

However,
it's looking more and more like,
it's feeling more and more like,
a fresh coat of paint on the wall.

Because even now. My thoughts find their way back
to you. So who are they really when,
at the root of it all
I see your eyes (sleek, blue, settled) before I sleep
when I wake, when I walk,
in my dreams.

Little Thoughts:

What if we didn't live in a linear time frame?

Maybe the question isn't which one is perfect for me
Maybe they're all perfect for me in their own way.
Touching on different unique attributes.

Perhaps no one is my true connection,
love of my life, the one and only, ultimate eternity.
For all one knows, in that moment of meet, that was
the love I needed, that was my split second soulmate

I think, love grows the same way we do.
We comprehend more as we age,
Therefore, we are able to love more too.

Love deepens with time.
                         & understanding.
Conclusively, love deepens as we learn
what it is to be loved. &
what is love and what is not

If I could go back this is how I would explain it to you now.

I loved you as much I could at the time.

Perhaps I'd love you more now,
love you more broadly now.

Or perhaps our moment has passed.

In the end, the beauty of this love is that it is cherished, and held permanently in that time of perfect bliss. Untainted by memories of unresolved quarrels and unkept promises.

The Glide.

Remember walking down those historic cobble stone streets.

The sun had set,
lights twinkled from shops.

Conversations coalescing
fading in and out of awareness.

Settling intoxication from
A post-skating thrill
Footsteps heavy,
had adjusted to gliding.

Charged.

Bustling crowds passing by was
a blur as you entwined our fingers.
My heart soared
and I told you,
right now,
I am overwhelmed with the beauty of this moment.

This was the second instance.

I miss you
I miss you
I miss you
I miss you
I miss you
I miss you
I miss you
I miss you
I miss you
I miss you
I miss you
I miss you
I miss you
I miss you
I miss you
I miss you
I miss you
I miss you
I miss you
I miss you
I miss you
I miss you
I miss you
I miss you
I miss you
I miss you
I miss you
I miss you
I miss you
I miss you
I miss you
I miss you
I miss you
I miss you
I miss you
I miss you

He was staring at her face when:

"What are you looking at?" She said.

"Just looking" He smiled.

He places his hands on each side of her cheeks, leaned her close and kissed her forehead.

Is this what it feels like to be loved ?

I think it was just
an arm,
loosely wrapped around my shoulders.
And I am hooked.

I have sunk.

Life is one endless resistance.

"Liberation" is a letting go of that resistance.

The sun cracks the horizon,
Light shatters across the land.
Rosy cheeks infused with a newly warmed glow.
A pulling breeze rises
and tugs with it the sounds of the wild.
The silent hum of cycling wheels glide along hard packed mud.
And aged eyes look beyond the rolling green kingdom. Graceful careless shoots.
A few steps south and your feet sinks into soft black sand. A dance of gritty imprints.
The vibrating crash of waves echoes through your bones. And you sway with each breath of a lifting current.

Oh the times of the past.
How they etch themselves into our memory.
Like carving on wood.

An island cold, desolate and awashed in snow.
A dull white crumbling scene. Dotted with rotting brown. Blizzards of dust swimming swiftly between shriveled palm trees.
A rattling cough rolls across the landscape,
A harsh escape from the lips of a stooped figure, too young to be shuffling with aching bones.

An archipelago sinking with the weight of an ice age.

Island. Ice breaks.
Snowfall adrift.
Days in sand. A winter wonderland.

Till Death Do Us (Part V).

She traipses along the edge of a cliff
The squawk of seagulls nearer
than the vibrating pound of a bass too loud.

She kicks
a rock
Watch as it flies and gravity drags it
smack
against the face of the cliff

Too late she acknowledges
she has followed it's path
Crunch
is her face smashed on a protruding rock
Crack
is her neck snapped across a jutted precipice
and then a high-pitched
Smack
is her body, sinking into the deep glittering ocean

The call of conversation pulls her back to the now.

When I'm unsure what to write,
I think,
about,
What completely and utterly drives me to the brink of insanity.

Hold this head heavy myself
Do not spill into another soul.

Too young we found each other.
Both on the brink of something more.

Resentment.

I regret what I wrote about you.
But I guess that's part of the growth.

For how would I have known—
what it's like to feel special, to feel like the only one
you call the one, while you plan your days with
other ones.
—if it wasn't for you?

Someone told me, like any man, you only cast a
message to test the waters, see if I am still falling for
a bait you can't wait to reel in.

And not, because you're thinking of me, because
you care about me, because you want me.

I am not that easy.

I am not one of your women.
One in your list of women.
A checkpoint, a goal,
something to cross off,
to toss out when done.

I will not hold my life for a man who cannot decide.
If he wants me, or
If he wants me not.

Living in Times Square.

Every night the sounds of the night float up.
Through the glass of my window I hear

The orchestra of car horns

Sirens singing in and out

The sweet smooth melodic notes of a single
saxophone
I hum myself to sleep.

People laughing
People yelling
Scattered Speeches of the Sober
Passionate Pleas of the Plastered

And I think
This.
This is the New York of people's fairytales.

Living in My Island Home.

The lingering day turns its face and a pink sky fades
into a navy blue canvas.
Decorated,
in the shattered sparkle of the stars.

The sounds of the evening sinks
and rises now a cacophony of the night.

Oh to be in love with the changing colours of the
skies, the elegant comfort of the trees, and caressing
whispers of the breeze.

To love like this, in love with the Universe,
is one never ending wave of bliss.

Fisherman Friend.

You said "thanks C" and in that moment
Everything we once shared came floating back to
me.

Remember the way we talked
The way we argued

The way you wanted to pull your hair out
The way you loved me

It's a lovely feeling to reminisce, but don't do it so
you fall in love with the thought of someone's
identity in your perception, and not who they
actually were.

Because remember how you turned to the warmth
between her legs and hers and hers.

The beam of smooth words you shone at me swung.
And it became a tool. instead of any real indication
of how you felt.

But when it came back I fell over and over and over,
tripping at the dark when the light shifted again.

Scraping bruises & denting scratches on my skin.
And still, you had me on the line.

I guess you were a fisherman after all.

I thought I broke your heart.
When I said goodbye.

But in the end,
Why is it my heart that
all the king's horses and all the king's men,
Are unable to put,
Back together again?

I like to think I am hurtling towards someone.

That some day,
    some time,
        some where,
            my collision is out there.

And I missed you.

I smile because no one else should have to feel this dark heaviness.

This mass of thickness holding down your chest, your head

This inability to make it disappear

This fleeting sense of happiness and a crashing drop lower as you realize,
it doesn't go away.

Lower and lower each time
Until
You just
.

The end.

Thank you for watching.
We hope you enjoyed the show.

How can we fully understand someone to what they want us to understand, ever?

We only grasp what they manage to convey, without clearly knowing if this is what they wished to convey the way it is in their head.

My blue is your blue but what you know as blue may be what I see as red. But we wouldn't know. That it is any different in our minds.
Our separate brains.

I can easily tell you that my heart feels heavy but your understanding of heavy is vastly different compared to mine.

For the woman who lost her unborn child, each day sits a battle in her heart, caging the torrent behind her eyes, holding a kitten and crumbling at the sight of its search for its mother.

Nothing else could be worse.

For the boy who is locked in an endless war inside his mind. The alluring call of a noose around his neck clashing against the urge to pick up the phone and cry out for help. He doesn't want to die. He doesn't want to live. He cannot contain his pain in this empty vessel.

Anything else would be better.

You see, how can we compare? How can we understand?

Till Death Do Us (Part VI).

She is a guest
in her own home.
Her life under
the life
being carved through
the wood
on her doors,
her roof,
the very foundation of the house.

She falls onto the couch and
the music of
splintering wood cracks
at her ears.

The roof crumbles.

Life above and
life below
meet in
a splayed display
against the white
tiled floor.

She wonders why she always finds her way back to death.

We finish each other's thoughts.

Not in the way that they are the same

My unfinished thoughts are brushed and packaged by him.

We complete each other's thoughts.

He brings in his own perspective that,

You see, it's like,

I have a draft in my head, and he makes it into a finished final piece. Does that make sense?

I am complete on my own, but with him, we glow differently. We are, a masterpiece.

To be with you.

An emotional reflection of who I am.

Would it be a breathe of fresh air?

Or like two anchors swirling deeper into the sea?

The loss of a person.

The pain, comes not from simply losing the person. It is the fact that this loss takes withs it all the parts of who you were with them. The parts of you that was found in being with them. An entire universe built in shared moments, in to-be shared moments, taken out of existence just like that.

This one is a tribute.

To the boy that lost his mother,

The man that lost his brother

The girl who lost a love,
The woman who lost a love,
before it was a life.

The ones who lose people, and still, go on living somehow.

It is not easy, to brush death off your shoulders, pick yourself up and carry on.

Somehow, we all do it anyway.

What a courageous group of humans we are.

I see her in my dreams.

Your eyes, my mouth.
Wind-swept sun-bleached gold-brown hair
Calculative, observant.
A wisdom deeper than ours combined.
A better version of the two of us.

A beach, empty.
She smiles with a roll of her eyes,
Tolerating,
She raised us. basically.

A photo, she's sandwiched between a me on her right and a you on her left.
We are loosely clasped together.
My arms wrapped tightly around her as I grin and she lifts a corner of her lips knowingly and your eyes, shinning the way they do.

Tilted, Hooded.
Mirrors.

I think perhaps she took more of you than me.
She insists that is not the truth.
We're two bodies sharing a soul.
How could she not be the whole.

I think perhaps she was my best friend.

Find me someone, where the conversation never runs dry.

And the moments of silence are buzzing.

I am the creator of my own limits.

They force you to forget about your magic
And with this, you forget about your worth.

Don't let them control you
Don't let them define and or set your limitations.

Living with a writer.
We notice such irrelevant details, don't we.

I won't remember your birthday, and to you this is an indication that I am, truly, the worst friend.

But I'll remember how you called me first thing when you found out your dog had been poisoned. How you could barely get the words out through the choked sobs. I was there in an instant. And we cried the night away.

I'll remember how you else told me to please check in on you. That you are, struggling, but you don't know how to say it. And you worry that if you simply disappeared, none of us would notice.
I promise, always.

And you, with hooded eyes you laugh about the things that make you collapse in sadness. No tears in your eyes but they are eyes shattered in a pain no one else can see. You are always there for every single person we know, and yet never ask for anything in return. Your words tell one story, but your downcast lids tell another. I have a shoulder to cry on, please feel free to use me.

This one had a different intent when I started, but it has become a tribute to my dearest friends. I know I'm the least capable of saying I love you, but from the depths of my heart, I love you all.
Almost as much as I love mint chocolate chip ice cream.

Bathe in this moment.

Allow me to stay here,
In this,

A little longer please.

Till Death Do Us (Part VII).

Was it her own
form of madness,
perhaps,

to think
of death as

a way of living?

My soul is careening to one, my heart jumps at all.

In a fairytale situation
The way I was told,
My soul should be pulling to one,

But my heart jumps at all hoping they are the one,
rationalizing they are the one,
convinced they are the one.

Is this what it is to be a hopeless romantic?
Or to be ridiculously naive?

Am I seeking for the one because I think they will fulfill me? Or because I lack fulfillment on my own terms?

Yes, I think that's it.

I wish so strongly to be completed, failing to understand I am of complete nature on my own.

There is only you here, and you are us. and us is we. and we is all and all is me. and I am you.

A fog has rolled in.
And nobody has noticed.

"Change begins with one step."

And another.
And another.
Until one day you glance up and
realize you are
at the top,
looking down.

There is one <u>thing</u> that inspires an artist.

The light of a candle against the wall:
soft fluttering. focused intent. fierce desire. warmth,
enveloped. a mother's love, a lovers embrace,
embraced by father, by God.

trauma:
the memory of him of what he did
is buried. deep.
intoxicated it is dark. alone. out. the music pulses.
throbbing head
it has resurfaced.

a moment in love:
"every time I say his name you can't even control
the smile— see, you're doing it again."

I can breathe
I can

I can't

I can

When will this cycle end.

head whirling, feet won't fly.

your head is peacefully sinking in rough waters

Little thoughts:

The dying of a light in one's eyes
when stabbed with indifference.

Souls A silhouette
Dark shadows
Flickering against rainbow beach

A foreigner in my own home.

Quiet
    Chaos.

Observation. Introspection.

somewhere.
>   nowhere.
>   >   always, no where

now here.

Jazz Jam.

Music that seeps through skin through heart and skims on soul.

Vibrations in your chest and a swing in your limbs.

An unavoidable need to get up and throw yourself across the room.

He was
A thousand suns
shining
through his eyes.

The Flight.

Sun tapestry bed sheets bright.
A yellow room in the concrete city.

I lay next to you and I turned,
your eyes.
My heart dropped and hopped in one swift slice.

We spent the day testing time, like we could slow it down just by telling it to. Fabricating tales of a plane ride postponed.

This is the third instance, I knew.
Do I tell you? Do I tell you?

I held. The words, in my throat.

But then we were walking to the station.
We were sitting in the train.
We stepped into the last stop before our parting.
And we sat, lingering.

We talked about, nothing.
My head screaming, heart winking in and out of existence, wringing my fingers I could feel every particle of sweat forming on my palm of my hands.

"The things is"
"The thing is I"

You watching me with those unsettling deep
sea eyes.

"There's something I want to say, that I know if I don't say it I'll regret it."
"Now I know you might not feel the same but,"
I looked up. The curve of a smile on the left side of your lip.

"No," you said. "Just say it you never know,"

Your eyes playful, waiting, like a cat about to pounce. I wonder if you felt how each nerve sparked on my skin, high voltage in my head.

I don't remember what else I said building up to it, a lot of really unnecessary commentary, probably, all to build up the courage. But I do remember clearly saying, "And I think I'm in love with you."

A pause. "Whoo my whole body just felt that rush,"

And you looked at me, with that smile, and said "I love you too." And kissed me.

This was the instant when I told you.

"How did you know?"

"I don't know if I knew, knew."

"I had decided.
Yeah, I feel very happy when I see you,
and I really didn't want to leave you there and then,
so, it's more like I slid into something
and it clicked."

A sentence, comes into its full meaning once it has been concluded. At the point of the full stop.

Similarly, our life comes into meaning, at the end of its existence. In death.

Maybe that's why those who seek for meaning, choose to come to a close on their own terms.

Till Death Do Us (Part VIII).

She thought of death because it was the only way to prove she was still living. There are so many possibilities, so many ways to end a life.
Each breath could be the last, every moment precious.

poetry is therapy.
and this is my way of working through.

behold, my jumble of notes
tumble of thoughts

spewed out into this chaotic, restless,
no sense
of a space.

It is a motion staggered and hastened
simultaneously, when
lifted lashes dragging lids
and beneath reveals embers, eyes dark,
piercing,
peaceful, restrained.
They are deep, and undressing.
My chest erupts in a flutter of repressed passion.
It is, a provocation, temptation,
daring me —

And then, it hits the light
and rays of crystalline gold
leaves me
completely out of breath.
Brilliant, melting honey,
bottomless
a surface glassy as the waves blanketing our
horizon.
I am unravelled in a different way
suddenly, I want to be captivated,
eternally consumed in the embrace of your eyes.

Swedish late summers
In this august breeze
You glow.
Disheveled
Careless
We slug our way through the day as the sun refuses to set.

— — — —

8pm sunset swims
We're kids talking about our kids and
Romanticizing a future where,
It's not a two week, two month, two year kind of relationship.

— — — —

Lying on the rocks we reached for something more optimistic.
Fingers grabbing blindly, chaotically.
Anchoring on
Deep sea, unstable.
In the midst of it all,
We laughed at speech failure, and dreamed of candies and chocolate.

— — — —

My heart shrouds in steel, to think of an end.
But realistically, how long can we do this for?

Dad once asked me why I'm always writing about love

I didn't have an answer

Still don't have an answer

maybe love is the easiest thing to write about

Simple words on complex thought

And perhaps I'm not such a good writer after all.

You're there but you're not really there.

Your head is a whirlwind
And your lungs are filling with sand.

The buzz encircling your mind just keeps getting louder and louder
When will the heaviness end.

The water. The water is calming.
I'm thinking of all the ways to go.
In a pool, in a lake, in the sea so clean, serene,
in deep,
the breeze.
Is pulling me.
Seducing me.
It is telling me, that
The fear,
The moment, of,
The right before the end.
Is only temporary.

The same water occupying your lungs as you scream (involuntarily) will eventually be what cleanses you.

As you are enshrined in the
eternal peace of the dead.

Sometimes I think it might just be easier for me,
For all involved,
If I just left it all behind.

In my most soothing fantasies I am,
Walking along the edges of a lake.

The water breathing as it shrinks and expands,
The whispers of leaves brushing against each other,
as it moves with the wind,
And my head writhing,
So close to peace.

The water is cool and tranquilizing
as it hugs my feet, torso, chest
and suddenly
I am enveloped in its serenity.

There are rocks tied to my ankles and as it pulls me
deeper my breathing slows, and I am endless.
In being.

I am embraced by this an undisturbed clarity,
The final resting place,
My head, empty as it has ever been.
Finally.

You fall into passivity

Or slip into insanity.

A mother's love
Her love
Is love

An everlasting, unconditional type of care
For me, for you, for all ensnared

I use that, in positivity
For those fortunate enough to be in her vicinity

Because a cage, suffocation, it is not.

She loves like fleece blankets in winter
Like the blossoms in the spring

Her love is your surroundings
Her love, a fine caress.
The way it hugs you
Encompasses you

Like hot chocolate gliding down to your stomach.
It is a slow heartbeat, sure-footing
Forever comforting kind of love.

In this love you know, whatever fear whatever
darkness whatever tears you have,
She will tenderly hold you either way.

My Love for Chocolate Cake

Smooth to touch
Warm to taste
A velvet luscious lethargic dribble

Shimmering in your stance
You glow
A delicate softness
My mouth, against you
A feverish embrace,
A lavish devouring

One slice not enough
Two too many.

I cannot bear to be without you for long.

Dark is your nature
Sweet on my tongue.

I crave you endlessly,
religiously,

eternally trapped in your unparalleled divinity.

Uncluttered are my thoughts. For.

The alluring intensity of your eyes,
as you glide them interchangeably between
my lips and my eyes as I speak.
Is it simply habit, or an invite?

All I can see is the shape of your lips formulating
soft and structured words.
Suddenly I am overwhelmed by the shape of your
collarbones.
innocence. Sensual.
I am internally derailed. I have lost my footing in
what we are. What we are supposed to be

Should I cross this line?

Little thoughts:

Can you even go missing when there's no one to notice your loss?

Till Death Do Us (Part IX).

Death is the resistance that keeps one alive. It is symbiotic. How would one know to keep on living, if death was not looming in so near a distance?

In the old days
I could go to the beach and see almost no one.
Disconnect was a reality.

When seaweed coiled around our ankles
We plucked them off without a thought
It became a game, flinging their slimy remains away!

And now we wade in a sea crawling with a wide range of synthetic particles
Discomfort erupts as it slides course grease across our skin.

We slow circle our way through the waves and a whirlpool of plastic cups and plastic straws and plastic packets of chips shadow us.

We walk the sandy horizon in a drunken zigzag path, as a way to avoid the crowd, the crowd, the endless crowd.

When did home become so suffocating?

If the sea has a bed, would that not imply that we could lay there, in an eternal slumber

The waves washing away all thought, form, and any indication of your existence.

Wouldn't the water be a good way to go?

Besides the screaming of your lungs, it would be nice to be peacefully submerged

in the rolling cool
the rumbling blue
of the deep salty sea.

consent.

The way a heart shatters,
Is the way a silent sob fractures into the shudder of a woman defeated.
A woman who has placed the fullness of her onto another who did not have the capabilities to see the divinity within her.

A broken heart is
Aimless reaching
Sliding your fingers across a flesh newly opened,
A knife wound.
You dig, you dig
Until suddenly, it hurts

And she is sobbing on the bathroom floor

A heart crumbling the way a building topples onto the ground.
A scorching crash, a searing tumble.

There is no end in sight.

The kindness instilled in you,
That ebbs from you
Ripples unto, across, the world.

I can tell you're a person that is always happy
- someone once said to me.

Why do I look that way?
I used to feel, unmatched in this description.

I felt, deceived.
Deceived in the way one feels when you are wearing a mask, but you still hope they see the pain behind it.

I felt anger, that people only see what they want to see. But what is the matter with looking happy?

Isn't that good?

Isn't that good, if they think you're happy?

The sun plunges and the sky erupts in a tumbling scatter of colours. Your breath is drawn out of your lungs, as you are absorbed by its beauty, its everlasting ability to present a new canvas every day. Holding impermanence as a constant state. You fail to see a reflection of this beauty gracing any part of you. But my darling, there is love pouring out of your heart. Kindness shining through your eyes, an elegant softness radiates from your hands, your skin, your being. Your light dazzles and warms those around you. How can you not see, the divinity within you?

In love's eternal embrace, we prosper.
Only through friction,
Disagreements,
And entirely different perspective crashing against your own, can we grow.
The endless journey towards our ultimate self.

We are, at the end of it, the product of those we've crossed paths with.

There's no sense
There's no sense
in anything
in our purpose
in our final soul clash?

Were you the one?

Beachside.

How is something simultaneously a rageous beast
and a gentle cradle at once.

A curl that pulverizes and kisses the submitting
sand in one motion.

It is occurring, not parallel, but, at the same time.

One being two parts.

Maybe, we should follow in this example.
Maybe, this is what is theorized when one soul splits
as two beings.

Living not parallel to each other, but as one motion
at once
happening concurrently.

It was charged.
The moment, was charged.
You sat there, in the calmness of breath.
And here I was uncoiled in the electricity of your presence
In the background is the thought
What if?

Feeling the uninspired life consuming me.

There's a lack of poetic wonder within me.

Maybe,
because, for awhile,
    I've been happy.

I should've written more while
I was hurting from you.
Because now that I have moved on,
it's hard to write about
how shattered I was.

I think it was necessary for me to be completely
broken in that way.
To discover what true happiness means.

It is the act of letting go.

It hurts to discover, the lie a lover tells.

It hurts even more, having known the truth,
and watching them lie straight to your face.

This love you show for her,
I hear in the words you say to me.
But I can't do anything with your words,
When she has all your heart.

mother mother i am here,
mother, i am here
i am here, mother,
i am hurting
mother mother
see me
my hand, my hand mother
i am out at sea,
i am out
i am out in the middle of
a whirlpool,
mother,
a whirlpool I am under
see me
mother, my hand, mother
my hand is reaching
take me. take me. take me.
mother, i am out in the middle of a whirlpool please
help me,
i am here, i am here,
i am so alone,
mother i am spinning, mother.
i am spinning.
i am spinning i am spinning
i am spinning.
endless
endless
endlessly
mother,
Help me.

<u>Till Death Do Us (Part X).</u>

And with these parting words she dies.

And yet, as Shakespeare would say, she is as eternal as these words.

Oh my love.

You are a Phoenix.

Acknowledgements

Here is where I would just like to say a quick thank you to a few of my friends for helping me make this book a possibility.
To Will for making a png version of the cover because I am not great with electronic and design.

To Natasha for helping me edit some of it despite our different preferences.

And to Bali's Baddest for helping me with some thoughts and notes on a few of the pieces.

And of course all the people in my life who continue to believe in me and my writing and continue to support me through it all.

Thank you, and much love.

Printed in Great Britain
by Amazon